Salvation

The Most Important Thing in the World!

Folo Ajibade

Dedication

I dedicate this book to God Almighty, the father of our Lord Jesus Christ, my God, my father and our father in heaven, who has given me the privilege, grace and the direction to write this book letting the world to note the most important thing in the world.

I dedicate this book to Jesus Christ the head of the church, my Lord, my master and redeemer who humbled himself to die for us all so as to be saved and giving us the hope of eternal life that awaits us in paradise for a world without end with the father.

I dedicate this book to the Holy Spirit my guide, my comforter, my all in all for giving me such inspiration and guidance for writing this book.

Preface

The aim of this book is to point people to what salvation is and why it is the most important thing in the world.

The word man used in this book is a general wording referring to both men and women.

The scriptures references used are from the King James Version (KJV).

Contents

What is Salvation ?

In theology, salvation is the deliverance from sin and its consequences, believed by Christians to be brought about by faith in Christ. Whereas in general meaning according to the dictionary, It is the preservation or deliverance from harm, ruin, or loss. With the combination of the two definitions above whether according to theology or general meaning, it is clear that anything that can deliver from sin and its consequences, harm, ruin or loss must be a very important thing. For instance, the bible says the consequence or wages of sin is death according to Romans 6:23 which says:

For the wages of sin is death; but the gift of God is eternal life through Jesus Christ our Lord.

Salvation is the gift and eternal plan of God for mankind to save us from the destruction that is coming ahead upon the world or life beyond this physical realm. In the beginning when God created man, he commanded him what he should not do but that the day he disobey this commandment, he shall surely die. What is this commandment ? Let us look at Genesis 2:16:

And the Lord God commanded the man, saying, Of every tree of the garden thou mayest freely eat: But of the tree of the knowledge of good and evil, thou shalt not eat of it: for in the day that thou eatest thereof thou shalt surely die.

We know that it is impossible for God to lie (Numbers 23:19). He is the only personality that can never lie, has never lied and will never lie because all his words are yea and amen according to 2 Corinthians 1:20:

For all the promises of God in him are yea, and in him Amen, unto the glory of God by us.

If God is a liar, then there would have been no God. But what makes him God is his "holiness". He is absolutely pure and holy and that is why his heavenly hosts call him "holy" day and night without rest according to Revelation 4:8 which says:

And the four beasts had each of them six wings about him; and they were full of eyes within: and they rest not day and night, saying, Holy, holy, holy, Lord God Almighty, which was, and is, and is to come.

We all know that God is so powerful from the wonders of his creations of things we can see like the sky, the seas and oceans, all kinds of animals, rocks, mountains, vegetations, times and seasons, different weather and much more things we cannot see with our eyes. His heavenly hosts could have been saying, *powerful, powerful, powerful, Lord God Almighty, which was, and is, and is to come.* But his holiness is his highest nature that makes him God and that is why he cannot lie and will never lie. The bible says in Numbers 23:19 that:

God is not a man, that he should lie;
neither the son of man, that he should repent

He has never lied and will never lie neither does he has any lie to repent from. Now this absolute holy God who can never lie commanded man in the beginning of creation that the day he eats from a particular tree, he would surely die. Unfortunately man was deceived by the devil which is Satan the fallen angel in form of a serpent and made the woman (Eve) who was Adam's wife to eat of the forbidden tree. She gave some to her husband (Adam) also and by doing this, something happened in the spirit realm which is still the problem of mankind till today thus why salvation is needed. Let us look at the book of Genesis 3:1-7:

Now the serpent was more subtil than any beast of the field which the Lord God had made. And he said unto the woman, Yea, hath God said, Ye shall not eat of every tree of the garden? And the woman said unto the serpent, We may eat of the fruit of the trees of the garden: But of the fruit of the tree which is in the midst of the garden, God hath said, Ye shall not eat of it, neither shall ye touch it, lest ye die. And the serpent said unto the woman, Ye shall not surely die: For God doth know that in the day ye eat thereof, then your eyes shall be opened, and ye shall be as gods, knowing good and evil. And when the woman saw that the tree was good for food, and that it was pleasant to the eyes, and a tree to be desired to make one wise, she took of the fruit thereof, and did eat, and gave also unto her husband with her; and he did eat. And the eyes of them both were opened, and they knew that they were naked; and they sewed fig leaves together, and made themselves aprons.

After the man and the woman the Lord God made in the beginning disobeyed God by eating from the forbidden tree commanded by God for them not to eat, they actually did died but this kind of death was not a physical death because of course they were still alive after eating the fruits. Because God cannot lie, they did died as he said. That kind of death was a spiritual one which disconnected man from God because man was actually created in the likeness of God. The likeness of God is that God is a Spirit according to John 4:23. That is why we cannot see God with our physical eyes until we transform totally to a spirit.

A man is a spirit being, he has a soul and he lives in the body. Remember we are created in the image and likeness of God according to Genesis 1:26-27:

And God said, Let us make man in our image, after our likeness: and let them have dominion over the fish of the sea, and over the fowl of the air, and over the cattle, and over all the earth, and over every creeping thing that creepeth upon the earth. So God created man in his own image, in the image of God created he him; male and female created he them.

Because God is a Spirit, and we are created in his image and likeness means we look like him physically according to his image and we look like him spiritually according to his likeness which is why we are all spirit being but having a soul and living in the body.

When man disobeyed God in the beginning, their spirit nature in the likeness of God died, there was a disconnection from God automatically till today from every man born and that is where the subject of salvation came in for God to restore man back to himself.

Salvation is God's provision for humanity to restore back the relationship he first had with mankind in the beginning. After the disobedience of Adam and Eve, sin was created into the world and we know that the wages of sin is death according to Romans 6:23, that death is a spiritual death and disconnection from God that is still the problem of the whole world till today. Everyone is born automatically into this nature of sin. That is why you don't teach a child to lie before you see that a little child who does not know these mystery automatically lies at some point in life and knows what is evil and what is not. This spiritual death makes man to automatically live in sin and that is where the subject of salvation comes in to be saved from our sins so as to return back to God our creator in spirit and in truth.

Salvation is God's love to rescue us so that we wont go to hell. Whether you believe it or not, there is heaven and there is hell. God wants you and I to spend eternity with him in heaven after our life on earth is over but this can only happen through his salvation and this salvation has been given to us only through his son, Jesus Christ.

After the fall of man in the garden of Eden where the relationship of man and God broke, salvation is the only alternative God has created through his beloved son Jesus Christ to redeem man back to himself that whosoever believes in this simple mystery, they shall live forever with him in heaven and not go to hell.

In John 3:16, that popular verse of the scripture. It says:

For God so loved the world, that he gave his only begotten Son, that whosoever believeth in him should not perish, but have everlasting life.

Further in verse 17-18, the scriptures says:

For God sent not his Son into the world to condemn the world; but that the world through him might be saved.
He that believeth on him is not condemned: but he that believeth not is condemned already, because he hath not believed in the name of the only begotten Son of God.

Salvation is the redemption of our soul by faith in Christ Jesus which guarantees our place in eternity. It connects us back to God spiritually while still here on earth. It restores back the original relationship God purposed at the beginning with mankind.

Salvation is the only way to truly know God and his love for us through Jesus Christ his son. It is not a thing that can be ignored. Definitely, it is the most important thing in the world. Though we have many things important to us, nothing can be compared to salvation which determines the kind of life we will live either after death or when rapture happens any time.

Salvation is a choice. People choose to believe it by faith in Jesus Christ and that makes anyone to become saved or people also choose not to believe it and unfortunately they will end up in hell if they die without being saved.

Salvation belongs to believers in Jesus Christ. It belongs to those who have made up their mind to spend eternity in heaven and not in hell. Someone has said, until you are saved, you are not safe! Salvation guarantees our safety in God from the hand of the enemy called the devil.

Why is Salvation Necessary ?

SO AS TO ESCAPE HELL

Salvation is very necessary because without it, no one can escape hell.

The bible says in Hebrews 2:3 that:

How shall we escape, if we neglect so great salvation; which at the first began to be spoken by the Lord, and was confirmed unto us by them that heard him

If you are not saved or if you do not receive salvation in life before death, it is clearly written in the world of God that hell cannot be escaped.

In a normal sense, I don't think anyone who can think at all would like to go to hell if they really understand and believe that hell is real but it is certain that a person would go to hell if the subject of salvation and its requirements to comply with are ignored according to the word of God.

Many people or let me say unbelievers who don't see salvation as a necessary thing are either mind-blinded by the enemy the devil or they chose to intentionally ignore it while they have the chance to believe.

Let us look at 2 Corinthians 4:3-4 which says:

But if our gospel be hid, it is hid to them that are lost: In whom the god of this world hath blinded the minds of them which believe not, lest the light of the glorious gospel of Christ, who is the image of God, should shine unto them.

I believe many would say "it does not matter" "it does not matter" until when they die without being saved and found themselves in hell to now realise that it really matters. Many must have gone to hell this way unintentionally while I believe many must have gone to hell intentionally by just taking the issue unserious or peradventure maybe they are too used to the subject to the point of still missing it in life. I pray that would never be your portion.

Therefore,

Be sober, be vigilant; because your adversary the devil, as a roaring lion, walketh about, seeking whom he may devour

Don't allow the enemy to blindfold you from receiving salvation into your soul.

But let us, who are of the day, be sober, putting on the breastplate of faith and love; and for an helmet, the hope of salvation.

1 Thessalonians 5:8

Another word for salvation or being saved is "Born Again"

I personally believe that salvation is the most important thing in the world because it guarantees our eternal life with God. Knowing that this life we are living is a temporary one here on earth, but there is a continuation of life forever after death or if Jesus comes back any time as promised. That second life is more important than the one we are living now because it is eternal and unending. That is why receiving salvation will determine your life and my life to spend with God in heaven for eternity or for those who reject it, a regretful life to spend in hell definitely awaits them.

In John 3:1-3.

There was a man of the Pharisees, named Nicodemus, a ruler of the Jews: The same came to Jesus by night, and said unto him, Rabbi, we know that thou art a teacher come from God: for no man can do these miracles that thou doest, except God be with him. Jesus answered and said unto him, Verily, verily, I say unto thee, Except a man be born again, he cannot see the kingdom of God.

So, answering the question of why is salvation necessary is simply to be able to see or enter into the kingdom of God at the end of this physical life. Jesus said clearly that except a man be born again, he cannot see the kingdom of God. That is very serious!. Can we argue with Jesus the direct son of God ? No! So no matter who you are and no matter what you have, if you are not born again or saved, you can never enter into the kingdom of God.

Jesus said in Matthew 16:26 that:

For what is a man profited, if he shall gain the whole world, and lose his own soul? or what shall a man give in exchange for his soul?

Salvation is a must and the most important thing in the world in all sense.

From my personal experience, I have ministered to people before about salvation and all they told me was that going to heaven is not necessarily by salvation through Jesus Christ but by the virtue of good deeds they do on earth. I saw people who have been really deceived by the devil. These kind of people are blindfolded by Satan and it will take the power of God for them to be delivered out of such bondage.

If you want to go to heaven and spend eternity with God, salvation is a must with no option. I believe those who rejected this truth while they had the opportunity in life before death are now regretting in Hell. I pray that this would not be your portion in Jesus' name.

One of the amazing testimony of salvation I ever heard in my entire life is that of my revered mentor in faith Kenneth E. Hagin of blessed memory even in his death but alive with Christ in heaven now, his own salvation experience was an interesting story for people to really listen to as he practically died in real life according to his testimonies and descended to Hell. But God in his exceptional mercy delivered him from hell such that he came back to life after dying 3 times within few minutes. He described how he was so close to entering into hell with the devil dragging him towards the gates of hell during his death without being born again but God saved him 3 times to come back to life after which he now finally confessed all his sins, the Lordship of Jesus and became born again or saved. He was a church goer as a teenager like many people do today, but he was not really born again. So going to church or practising church activities does not mean that you are saved. You need to be really born again to be able to enter into the kingdom of God and not go to Hell.

I remember ministering to a lady recently in Israel at the very front of Jesus' tomb about salvation and being born again but despite this lady being a Christian and practising all the religious activities at this pilgrimage, when I asked her about the issue of being born again, she was denying that truth. I was surprised! Many people are still blindfolded despite being Christians and deceiving themselves. I doubt what they claim to believe if they cannot follow the instructions that Jesus gave in the scriptures about entering the kingdom of God.

But thank God we have the power of choice given to us by God by the help and conviction of the Holy Spirit to be able to walk out on the devil. I don't know about you, but I chose to believe the truth of salvation and that is why I know I am saved when I gave my life to Jesus Christ years ago because I know it is necessary for me to enter into the kingdom of God at the end of life through salvation.

It is so necessary that God had to send his one and only begotten son Jesus into the world just for this specific and only purpose. Over 2000 years ago, Jesus came into the world for this only one reason to save mankind. Why ? because it is very necessary so that we can escape hell.

Nothing else was enough to redeem us from for our sin before God.

Neither is there salvation in any other: for there is none other name under heaven given among men, whereby we must be saved.

Acts 4:12

For God hath not appointed us to wrath, but to obtain salvation by our Lord Jesus Christ, Who died for us, that, whether we wake or sleep, we should live together with him.

1 Thessalonians 5:9

How to be saved

Be Humble

If you are not saved yet, for you to be saved, you first of all have to be humble before God. When people are saying there is no God or that they don't believe in God, those are all form of pride. A proud person cannot be saved! You need humility of heart to receive the salvation God has prepared for humanity through Jesus Christ. It is written that:

But he giveth more grace. Wherefore he saith, God resisteth the proud, but giveth grace unto the humble.

James 4:6

If you feel too big for God, you cannot be saved! Many people must have gone to hell I believe because of their pride to receive salvation. From the scripture above, I will call that second "grace" "salvation". Meaning:

"...God resisteth the proud, but giveth salvation unto the humble".

It takes humility of the heart to be saved. That is, you may hear about the gospel witnessed to you or reading it as it is in this book and you humble yourself to believe and receive it. It is as simple as that. The Lord God says in Isaiah 45:22 that:

Look unto me, and be ye saved, all the ends of the earth:
for I am God, and there is none else.

You need to look unto God for it with all humility of the heart and just receive it when the opportunity shows up such as reading this book.

Believe

You need to believe for it to happen. The bible says:

He that believeth and is baptized shall be saved; but he that believeth not shall be damned.

Mark 16:16

What makes a believer in Jesus Christ to be called a believer is simply because he/she believes in him. A believer is someone who believes in something and our belief in Jesus Christ is what makes us to receive salvation. Nobody in a normal sense would like to be damned but as the word of the Lord says, he that believes not shall be damned. Choose to believe in Jesus Christ as the son of God.

Jesus himself said in John 10:9 that:

I am the door: by me if any man enter in, he shall be saved, and shall go in and out, and find pasture.

Jesus is saying that he is the door to salvation. This door is only one of its kind as there is no any other door to go in.

Neither is there salvation in any other: for there is none other name under heaven given among men, whereby we must be saved.
Acts 4:12

He also said: ...*I am the way, the truth, and the life: no man cometh unto the father, but by me.*
John 14:6

There was a scenario when the apostles of Jesus were in the prison.

And at midnight Paul and Silas prayed, and sang praises unto God: and the prisoners heard them. And suddenly there was a great earthquake, so that the foundations of the prison were shaken: and immediately all the doors were opened, and every one's bands were loosed. And the keeper of the prison awaking out of his sleep, and seeing the prison doors open, he drew out his sword, and would have killed himself, supposing that the prisoners had been fled. But Paul cried with a loud voice, saying, Do thyself no harm: for we are all here. Then he called for a light, and sprang in, and came trembling, and fell down before Paul and Silas, And brought them out, and said, Sirs, what must I do to be saved? And they said, Believe on the Lord Jesus Christ, and thou shalt be saved, and thy house.
Acts 16:25-31

Until you believe in the Lord Jesus Christ, you cannot be saved. The main reason why people don't make heaven is because of their rejection of Jesus Christ. When people don't believe in him, they can never be saved. Some people don't even want to hear the name of Jesus at all. It is like they were born as his enemy. Even from my personal experience of walking round the streets of Bethlehem the birth place of Jesus, all the way down to Jerusalem, Galilee, Capharnaum, Nazareth and round Israel, i could see everywhere in all these places that despite all these areas being historic places where Jesus himself lived and walked, many people living in all these areas still don't believe in him despite all evidence live and direct as they are written in the scriptures but all these are notwithstanding to them. What a people!

Confess and Repent

To be saved, you need to confess all your sins and genuinely repent from them. Confession is a formal statement admitting that one is guilty of something while repentance is a sincere regret or remorse for something and to make a U-turn from that thing is my own definition. Therefore to confess and repent is to admit that you are a sinner, guilty of sin and every bad things you may have done in life, feel regretful of them and make a U-turn unto God for the salvation of your soul.

Let us look at what the scriptures says about this

But what saith it? The word is nigh thee, even in thy mouth, and in thy heart: that is, the word of faith, which we preach; That if thou shalt confess with thy mouth the Lord Jesus, and shalt believe in thine heart that God hath raised him from the dead, thou shalt be saved. For with the heart man believeth unto righteousness; and with the mouth confession is made unto salvation.

Romans 10:8-10

From the scriptures above, we can see that confession is necessary for you to obtain salvation from God. This is very important.

The bible also says:

He that covereth his sins shall not prosper:
but whoso confesseth and forsaketh them shall have mercy.

Proverbs 28:13

You want to prosper in life and especially to obtain mercy from God ? confessing and forsaking your sins is necessary and its part of obtaining his salvation also.

But Why ?

All these confessions, believing and forsaking are all necessary because if you really want to go to heaven, you have to accept God's terms and conditions on this matter as it is non negotiable.

You don't argue with your landlord or landlady about his or her terms and conditions to rent a house. You either take it or leave it. You can't argue with your employer about the rules, terms and conditions laid out for your employment contract but you will either accept it to be employed or not. So what makes you think you can argue this matter with God your creator who is the most high whom no one can query on whatsoever he does. He is God and these are his terms and conditions for whosoever is interested of going to heaven. The wise will accept it while the fools will despise this truth to regret later when they die and found themselves in hell as many have done. You and I cannot change the rules God has laid down in his word about the terms of entering into heaven. Have you not read from his word that says:

Know ye not that the unrighteous shall not inherit the kingdom of God? Be not deceived: neither fornicators, nor idolaters, nor adulterers, nor effeminate, nor abusers of themselves with mankind, Nor thieves, nor covetous, nor drunkards, nor revilers, nor extortioners, shall inherit the kingdom of God.

1 Corinthians 6:9-10

The word of God is just so clear about salvation and it is those who embrace them that would be saved. One day, a lady came to my office on an appointment for counselling and I asked her if she was a Christian and she said yes. I asked her also about if she really wants to go to heaven and she said she knows she would go to heaven. Then I asked her further questions to see what she might be missing and found out that she drinks. She was a drunkard. I have never seen this kind side of the world before where so many women drink in my life. From where I came from, it was more common among some men, but here in the west, even a young teenage female knows how to get drunk. Anyway, I showed her the scriptures above that says even drunkard cannot make heaven and she was amazed to see that. I gave her the counselling she wanted and we prayed a simple prayer together and she left hoping that she would not drink again from that day onward.

You see, we just have to show people these truths of the scriptures especially unbelievers and even growing up Christians that are not matured enough in the faith but:

How then shall they call on him in whom they have not believed? and how shall they believe in him of whom they have not heard? and how shall they hear without a preacher? And how shall they preach, except they be sent? as it is written, How beautiful are the feet of them that preach the gospel of peace, and bring glad tidings of good things!

Romans 10:14-15

So then faith cometh by hearing, and hearing by the word of God.

Romans 10:17

When you hear the word of God preached to you, your faith builds up and comes alive or when you read from an inspirational book such as this where God has revealed his word to some level in the lives of authors of Christian books and literature, your faith will build up also and your eyes get opened to the truth. These are ways how people get saved. You don't get saved by reading books on things that are not true, fictions, stories, dreams or fairy tales. You get saved by aligning yourself to the word of God either by hearing or reading Christian book like this. Therefore be careful of what you read and listen to. Anything that does not have anything to do with God and his kingdom which are the most important thing in the world through salvation are not just worth listening to or reading as I count all such as waste of time and waste of destiny. Invest your time on things that really matter and if there is anything that matters most in this world, it is the salvation of the soul of mankind.

Can God forgive me ?

Emphatically yes! God would forgive anyone no matter whatever he/she has done in life as long as a genuine repentance is acted. The Lord says in his word that:

The soul that sinneth, it shall die. The son shall not bear the iniquity of the father, neither shall the father bear the iniquity of the son: the righteousness of the righteous shall be upon him, and the wickedness of the wicked shall be upon him. But if the wicked will turn from all his sins that he hath committed, and keep all my statutes, and do that which is lawful and right, he shall surely live, he shall not die. All his transgressions that he hath committed, they shall not be mentioned unto him: in his righteousness that he hath done he shall live. Have I any pleasure at all that the wicked should die? saith the Lord God: and not that he should return from his ways, and live?

Ezekiel 18:20-23

It is important to know that there is forgiveness with God. He is willing to forgive whosoever that would repent and forsake their sins or wicked ways.

There was this story of when Jesus was being crucified on the cross in the midst of two criminals:

And one of the malefactors which were hanged railed on him, saying, If thou be Christ, save thyself and us. But the other answering rebuked him, saying, Dost not thou fear God, seeing thou art in the same condemnation? And we indeed justly; for we receive the due reward of our deeds: but this man hath done nothing amiss. And he said unto Jesus, Lord, remember me when thou comest into thy kingdom. And Jesus said unto him, Verily I say unto thee, Today shalt thou be with me in paradise.

Luke 23:39-43

Paradise is Heaven. From the above scriptures, even at the point of death at the last minutes for these two criminals to die for their sins and heading for hell, Jesus saved one of them who was wise enough to humble himself and pleaded for mercy that Jesus should remember him in his Kingdom. And how amazing was the response of our master Jesus, he promised him paradise meeting the same day, meaning he was saved at the last minute. I guess the other crook that accused the master Jesus didn't make heaven that day because of his pride which is the same thing many people are practising today by not yielding themselves to God for salvation.

When Can I Decide ?

Now! Tomorrow may be too late. Nobody knows tomorrow. Since you and I don't know what next even in the coming one hour time talkless of tomorrow, wisdom demands that you make your decision now today.

The bible says:

We then, as workers together with him, beseech you also that ye receive not the grace of God in vain. (For he saith, I have heard thee in a time accepted, and in the day of salvation have I succoured thee: behold, now is the accepted time; behold, now is the day of salvation.)

2 Corinthians 6:1-2

Salvation is not something to joke with or postpone. Many have postponed the day of their salvation when the had the chance to surrender their lives to Jesus but never see the next day. Someone has said "opportunity once lost is forever lost" I do not totally agree with that. Peradventure maybe you had the chance before and heard about all these before and never believe or yield yourself to Jesus for salvation of your soul but God is giving you another chance or opportunity today through this book to repent and turn to him for salvation. Since nobody knows tomorrow, is it not wisdom to surrender to Jesus today ?

Postponing salvation is a risk! You may never get this kind of chance again to turn to Jesus for the salvation of your soul. That bible passage above says *...now is the day of salvation*

"Salvation is a matter of urgency and something to make haste about"

There was this story about Zacchaeus in Luke 19: 1-9:

And Jesus entered and passed through Jericho. And, behold, there was a man named Zacchaeus, which was the chief among the publicans, and he was rich. And he sought to see Jesus who he was; and could not for the press, because he was little of stature. And he ran before, and climbed up into a sycomore tree to see him: for he was to pass that way. And when Jesus came to the place, he looked up, and saw him, and said unto him, Zacchaeus, make haste, and come down; for to day I must abide at thy house. And he made haste, and came down, and received him joyfully. And when they saw it, they all murmured, saying, That he was gone to be guest with a man that is a sinner. And Zacchaeus stood, and said unto the Lord; Behold, Lord, the half of my goods I give to the poor; and if I have taken any thing from any man by false accusation, I restore him fourfold. And Jesus said unto him, This day is salvation come to this house, forsomuch as he also is a son of Abraham.

For his haste to see Jesus our master and to repent of his wrong doings, Jesus did not postpone his salvation till another. He said to him *...this day is salvation come to this house.* You too can receive your salvation today and even right now. Yes right now if you believe it from your heart and confess it with your mouth, you will receive your salvation now.

PRAYER OF SALVATION

Are you wondering what a prayer of Salvation is ? It is the best and the greatest prayer you can ever pray in this world because it will secure your eternity in Heaven. That is, life after death. Peradventure many people don't know that there is life after death and think when you die, you just die like a dog and life ends there but that is not true. There is life after death called eternity. When you die, your body is buried or cremated but your spirit which is the real you living inside of you either goes up to Heaven back to God or it goes deep down below the earth into Hell fire to be with the devil called "Satan" who is the deceiver of the world from receiving the truth of God's salvation as written in the Bible.

The difference between people that go up to Heaven or Hell after death is simply this "Prayer of Salvation". It is all about believing in your heart first that, there is a God who is the Creator of Heaven and this Earth and that the whole world sinned from the beginning of creation through the first man and woman called Adam and Eve, but Thanks be to God, He made a provision of redemption and restoration of us back to himself through his only begotten son called "Jesus" that whosoever believes in him, serve him and follow him while still alive will have eternal life, everlasting life in Heaven with God. Satan who is the enemy of God knows this truth, therefore, he blocks peoples heart from believing this that they might be saved and escape Hell after their death. No mater who you are and no matter how bad you may think you are, God is ready to forgive you and receive you into his family but only through Jesus Christ our saviour who came to this world over 2000 years ago to die for us all, took away all our sins and redeemed us back to God but before we can receive this redemption into our spirit, we need to pray the prayer of salvation which is simply the confession of our belief in this truth which can never be changed by anyone. The Bible says in John 3 verse 16-18 that "*For God so loved the world, that he gave his only begotten Son, that whosoever believeth in him should not perish, but have everlasting life. For God sent not his Son into the world to condemn the world; but that the world through him might be saved.. He that believeth on him is not condemned: but he that believeth not is condemned already, because he hath not believed in the name of the only begotten Son of God",* That is, Jesus Christ.

So therefore, if you have not prayed this prayer of salvation before, now is the time for you to pray this most important prayer in the world and you will receive the forgiveness of God and be saved now so that when you leave this world one day, you can be sure of going to Heaven and not Hell. Brothers and Sisters, you can only go to Heaven only through this God's terms and not on your own terms or by any good thing you do in life. The only way to Heaven is found in Jesus Christ and he is ready to receive you today if only you pray this prayer of Salvation. If you are ready for this greatest change in your life, now simply pray this

" Jesus, I believe you are the son of God who came to die for me and rose from the dead on the third day for my redemption and justification.

I receive you into my life as my Lord and my Saviour, please forgive me all my sins and cleanse me with your blood shed for me on the cross of calvary.

Now I believe I am forgiven, I believe I am saved. I believe I am born again and I'm now a child of God. Thank you for saving me, Amen.

If you have just prayed that prayer, Congratulations ! You are now saved, born again and have become a child of God. You are welcome into the family of God's children. You now belong to the household of God.

For by grace are ye saved through faith; and that not of yourselves: it is the gift of God:

Ephesian 2:8

This is your greatest gift from God. Salvation!. That is why it is the most important thing in the world.

Now that you are saved

Now that you are saved or born again, you now belong to the household of God. You are now a member of God's family even while still living here on earth until we join him in heaven at the return of Jesus or after death.

Now that you are saved or born again, you are now a new creature. Many things you used to do before that are not godly will have to stop so that you can live a Christian life.

If you used to smoke, you have to stop it.

If you used to lie, you have to stop it.

If you used to fornicate, you have to stop it.

If you used to commit adultery, you have to stop it.

If you used to steal, you have to stop it.

The above among the most popular ones but the list is unending are some ungodly things to avoid now that you are saved.

The bible says:

Therefore if any man be in Christ, he is a new creature: old things are passed away; behold, all things are become new.

2 Corinthians 5:17

You need to know and believe that all things about you are now new like as if they never existed before. Being saved or born again is a spiritual experience and your physical body remains the same. But by faith, we believe we are saved and born again. It is the biggest miracle that can happen to anyone. In fact, we learnt that heaven rejoices over a soul that repent. Jesus said:

I say unto you, that likewise joy shall be in heaven over one sinner that repenteth, more than over ninety and nine just persons, which need no repentance.

Luke 15:7

Now that you are saved or born again, you are no more under the curse of the law but now qualify for the blessing of Abraham and able to receive the promise of the Spirit.

The scriptures says:
Christ hath redeemed us from the curse of the law, being made a curse for us: for it is

written, Cursed is every one that hangeth on a tree: That the blessing of Abraham might come on the Gentiles through Jesus Christ; that we might receive the promise of the Spirit through faith.

Galatians 3:13-14

Amazingly, these benefits or promises of the Spirit are listed for us as recorded in the book of Revelation 5:9-12 that:

And they sung a new song, saying, Thou art worthy to take the book, and to open the seals thereof: for thou wast slain, and hast redeemed us to God by thy blood out of every kindred, and tongue, and people, and nation; And hast made us unto our God kings and priests: and we shall reign on the earth.
And I beheld, and I heard the voice of many angels round about the throne and the beasts and the elders: and the number of them was ten thousand times ten thousand, and thousands of thousands; Saying with a loud voice, Worthy is the Lamb that was slain to receive power, and riches, and wisdom, and strength, and honour, and glory, and blessing.

This shows that we are already loaded after being saved or born again. We just need to claim all these promises by faith to enjoy them. We are redeemed or saved to enjoy power, riches, wisdom, strength, honour, glory and blessings in Christ Jesus.

Now that you are saved or born again, God has translated you and I into the kingdom of his dear son and delivered us from darkness.

Who hath delivered us from the power of darkness, and hath translated us into the kingdom of his dear Son: In whom we have redemption through his blood, even the forgiveness of sins

Colossians 1:13-14

Now that you are saved, it is clear from the above scriptures that you have received forgiveness of sins and redeemed through the blood of Jesus Christ our Lord.
Now that you are saved or born again, your name has been written into the book of life in heaven.

He that overcometh, the same shall be clothed in white raiment; and I will not blot out his name out of the book of life, but I will confess his name before my Father, and before his angels.

Revelations 3:5

Now that you are saved or born again, you belong to God spirit, soul and body.

For ye are bought with a price: therefore glorify God in your body, and in your spirit, which are God's.

1 Corinthians 6:20

However, now that you are saved, there are other very important steps you need to take to be rooted and grounded in faith. It does not just stop at salvation and returning back to your old lifestyles. You need to take further steps to complete your salvation and have a perfect Christian walk.

Once saved is not forever saved

Some preachers out there would tell you or you may hear them preach saying "once saved, you are forever saved" and that no matter what else you do after salvation, you are still saved. Don't listen to such preachers. Such teachings are influenced by the devil. Let us apply common sense to such preaching. So if someone after being saved begins to steal or murdering people, do you think such salvation is still valid ? emphatically no!

The scripture says clearly that:

"...work out your own salvation with fear and trembling"

Philippians 2:12b

Another says:

What shall we say then? Shall we continue in sin, that grace may abound? God forbid. How shall we, that are dead to sin, live any longer therein?

Romans 6:1

But when the righteous turneth away from his righteousness, and committeth iniquity, and doeth according to all the abominations that the wicked man doeth, shall he live? All his righteousness that he hath done shall not be mentioned: in his trespass that he hath trespassed, and in his sin that he hath sinned, in them shall he die.

Ezekiel 18:24

Therefore:

Little children, let no man deceive you: he that doeth righteousness is righteous, even as he is righteous.

1 John 3:7

The God of the old testament is the same God of the new testament. All scriptures are valid and nothing is irrelevant from every single verses and chapters of the scripture if not such preachers might as well scrap psalms 23 that says " the Lord is my shepherd, I shall not want" out of their lives and say the Lord is not their shepherd because all these are in the same old testaments like Ezekiel 18:24 above.

While it is good to know the certain date you got saved just like your date of birth, however if you feel you have missed it at any point, that is when rededication comes in to rededicate your life to Christ. I have done this several times in my life. Even in my prayers any day, any time, anywhere, I still confess Jesus Christ as my Lord and my Saviour afresh as often as possible for the assurance of my salvation. Don't let pride to make you lose eternity. Don't think since you got saved, you never commit any sin again in life. You may commit a sin unintentionally even in thoughts. That is why the bible says:

He that covereth his sins shall not prosper:
but whoso confesseth and forsaketh them shall have mercy.

Provers 28:13

Depart from iniquity

Now that you are saved you need to depart from sin and iniquity for this is the foundation of a believer and a Christian living. The bible says:

Nevertheless the foundation of God standeth sure, having this seal, The Lord knoweth them that are his. And, Let every one that nameth the name of Christ depart from iniquity.

2 Timothy 2:19

Jesus said:

Not every one that saith unto me, Lord, Lord, shall enter into the kingdom of heaven; but he that doeth the will of my Father which is in heaven. Many will say to me in that day, Lord, Lord, have we not prophesied in thy name? and in thy name have cast out devils? and in thy name done many wonderful works? And then will I profess unto them, I never knew you: depart from me, ye that work iniquity.

Matthew 7:21-23

Sanctification

Now that you are saved, living in holiness, purity and sanctification must be the order of the day. The scriptures says:

But of him are ye in Christ Jesus, who of God is made unto us wisdom, and righteousness, and sanctification, and redemption

1 Corinthians 1:30

For this is the will of God, even your sanctification, that ye should abstain from fornication: That every one of you should know how to possess his vessel in sanctification and honour

1 Thessalonians 4: 3-4

But we are bound to give thanks alway to God for you, brethren beloved of the Lord, because God hath from the beginning chosen you to salvation through sanctification of the Spirit and belief of the truth

2 Thessalonians 2:13

Now that you are saved, walk as children of light.

For ye were sometimes darkness, but now are ye light in the Lord: walk as children of light

Ephesians 5:8

In the next chapters, by the help of God, I have listed the next right steps to be taken according to the word of God so as to be rooted and grounded in faith and so as to perfect your salvation.

Get a Bible

The first thing i believe a new believer or a new convert needs to do is to get a bible. If you didn't have one before, try to get one immediately as this is God's word that will daily guide you as a Christian.

The bible is God's manual for humanity. It is his guide for us about how to live and operate as Christians. It shows who God is and makes you to understand how God operates.

The scriptures said in psalms 119:105 that :

Thy word is a lamp unto my feet,
and a light unto my path.

It is by God's word that we understand the things of the Spirit. It is impossible to really know God without studying his word. In fact, we understand from the bible that God and his word are one.

In the beginning was the Word, and the Word was with God, and the Word was God.
John 1:1

No one have seen God before, but we all know him through his word that we study by the help of the holy spirit who guides us to comprehend the mysteries behind the letters so as to gain masteries in life. As soon as the devil sees that you have become born again, he would try to launch different temptations to get you off track of what you have just committed to. But by following God's word, you would know what to do per time. This word of God will guide you in the love and fear of him so that you can be rooted and grounded in the faith. Many things will come your way in this troubled world, but by his word in you, you won't want to do what is wrong like the way you used to live before. That is why the scriptures says:

Wherewithal shall a young man cleanse his way?
by taking heed thereto according to thy word.
With my whole heart have I sought thee:
O let me not wander from thy commandments.
Thy word have I hid in mine heart,
that I might not sin against thee.
Psalms 119:9-11

Therefore to live a Christian life, the bible is a <u>must</u> to have and study daily to know God. I cannot remember a day passed where I don't study God's word in my life. It is a compulsory part of living daily as Christians. The bible is the written word of God.

Though it comes in different versions, get the one you feel you like and easily understand but the master teacher of the word of God is the holy spirit. So pray to him to guide you as you study the word of God for good understanding.

It is by studying his word that we show ourselves approved unto him. 2 Timothy 2:15 says:

Study to shew thyself approved unto God, a workman that needeth not to be ashamed, rightly dividing the word of truth.

As you study God's word daily, you will continue to grow in his knowledge. It is the truth that sets us free from many troubles in life and shows that we are the disciples of Jesus indeed as we continue to abide by it. The bible says:

Then said Jesus to those Jews which believed on him, If ye continue in my word, then are ye my disciples indeed; And ye shall know the truth, and the truth shall make you free.

John 8:31-32

Therefore, be faithful in abiding by his word and you will grow daily in your relationship with God the father, Jesus his son and the Holy Spirit. This word of God will also guide your relationship with other people around you and your daily living as a Christian.

Join a Church

It is important to join a local church around you where you can fellowship together with other believers of Jesus Christ. There are all kinds of churches out there but make sure that the church is a bible-believing and bible-practising. There are some churches nowadays where they do not practise the things of the bible properly or where people are being misled. So you need to be careful of the kind church you join but in most cases, churches of Jesus Christ practice his word.

A church is not a social gathering where people just come to have fun, chats or catch up with friends but a spiritual gathering of God's people. The bible says in the book of Hebrews 12:22-23 that:

But ye are come unto mount Sion, and unto the city of the living God, the heavenly Jerusalem, and to an innumerable company of angels, To the general assembly and church of the firstborn, which are written in heaven, and to God the Judge of all, and to the spirits of just men made perfect.

When we gather at church, we are gathered in the city of the living God. It is our heavenly Jerusalem with the innumerable of company of angels. The church belongs to Jesus Christ. That is why it is a special place of gathering unto God to worship him together with other God's Children. Whenever you are in the church where the name of Jesus is called and worshipped, be rest assured that Jesus himself is there. He affirmed this in Matthew 18:20 that:

For where two or three are gathered together in my name, there am I in the midst of them.

Because he is not a liar, he is definitely always there in the gathering of his people. Though you may not see him with your physical eyes, but he is surely there.

When you are in church, you are taught the word of God apart from your daily study and fellowship with God and this gives you more spiritual strength. The scriptures says in psalms 84:7 that:

They go from strength to strength,
every one of them in Zion appeareth before God.

The word Zion actually means the church from Hebrews 12:22-23. When we go there, we appear before God in fellowship with his son Jesus Christ. So find a local church for this would help you to grow together with other believers of Jesus Christ. It must be a church where the word of God is preached undiluted as this will help your faith apart from your personal fellowship with the Lord. Fellowship with other believers is good as we can make friends with other believers and share the word of God together.

Questions can be asked about things not clear enough to you in the scriptures and you can be able to get help and comfort from your church family when you need one. In fact, Hebrews 10:25 admonishes us:

Not forsaking the assembling of ourselves together, as the manner of some is; but exhorting one another: and so much the more, as ye see the day approaching.

So find a local church to join today if you have not joined one.

Get Baptized

Now that you are saved or born again, it is very important to get baptized also. It is the instruction of Jesus about one of the requirements to enter into the kingdom of God. The scripture says in John 3:5 that:

Jesus answered, Verily, verily, I say unto thee, Except a man be born of water and of the Spirit, he cannot enter into the kingdom of God.

From the above scriptures, there are two kinds of baptisms we need to pass through before we can enter into the kingdom of God according to the words of Jesus. The first one is baptism in water by immersion. Jesus himself demonstrated this by getting baptized in water. Let us see the scriptures below:

Then cometh Jesus from Galilee to Jordan unto John, to be baptized of him. But John forbad him, saying, I have need to be baptized of thee, and comest thou to me? And Jesus answering said unto him, Suffer it to be so now: for thus it becometh us to fulfil all righteousness. Then he suffered him. And Jesus, when he was baptized, went up straightway out of the water: and, lo, the heavens were opened unto him, and he saw the Spirit of God descending like a dove, and lighting upon him: And lo a voice from heaven, saying, This is my beloved Son, in whom I am well pleased.

Matthew 3:13-17

Since Jesus said we too need to be baptized in water to enter into the kingdom of God, then we really need to. If he needed it himself to fulfil all righteousness, then we have no excuse. From my experience of talking to people about if they have been baptized or not, some have claimed that they were christened while as a baby and that it was their water baptism. This kind of belief as water baptism is wrong. That is simply a kind of dedication of the baby to God and not water baptism. It has to be by immersion in water to be a proper water baptism signifying being dead and raised up together with Christ as recorded in Romans 6:3-4 that:

Know ye not, that so many of us as were baptized into Jesus Christ were baptized into his death? Therefore we are buried with him by baptism into death: that like as Christ was raised up from the dead by the glory of the Father, even so we also should walk in newness of life.

That is when we are born of water.

The second kind of baptism is of the Spirit. This is when we are baptized in the Holy Spirit with the evidence of speaking in tongues or an unknown tongue as the Spirit gives us utterance. The scriptures says:

And when the day of Pentecost was fully come, they were all with one accord in one place. And suddenly there came a sound from heaven as of a rushing mighty wind, and it filled all the house where they were sitting. And there appeared unto them cloven tongues like as of fire, and it sat upon each of them. And they were all filled with the Holy Ghost, and began to speak with other tongues, as the Spirit gave them utterance.

Acts 2:1-4

Remember:
Jesus answered, Verily, verily, I say unto thee, Except a man be born of water and of the Spirit, he cannot enter into the kingdom of God.

John 3:5

This is very important also because Jesus said so. In fact, without the baptism in the Holy Spirit with the evidence and ability to speak in tongues or an unknown tongue, there would be some benefits missing that a person should be enjoying as a Christian because we speak mysteries to God when we are speaking in tongues or in an unknown tongue as recorded in 1 Corinthians 14:2 that:

For he that speaketh in an unknown tongue speaketh not unto men, but unto God: for no man understandeth him; howbeit in the spirit he speaketh mysteries.

It takes the baptism in the Holy Spirit to be able to speak in tongues or in an unknown tongue. I cannot remember a day that passed by without me speaking in tongues or in an unknown tongues. When I wake up in the morning, I like to speak in tongues, when I do my prayers, I like to speak in tongues and any time anywhere, I open this fire because I understand that I am speaking mysteries unto God and not unto men.

So now that you are saved or born again, make sure that you get baptized in the Spirit also for your benefits and for your access into the kingdom of God as Jesus said. It is very important. Many churches practise these two baptisms. But if they do not, you can find your way into somewhere else that practise them to get baptized in water. You can pray your way into getting baptized in the Holy Spirit and it can happen by the hand of God on you as Jesus is the one that baptize in the Holy Spirit (John1.33). There are testimonies of such.

Therefore get baptized!

Be Prayerful

Now that you are saved or born again, you will need to be prayerful because the devil your enemy is always on the look about how to bring you down or cause you to sin either through temptations or through your fellow humans. We are admonished in 1 Peter 5:8 to:

Be sober, be vigilant; because your adversary the devil, as a roaring lion, walketh about, seeking whom he may devour:

Jesus also said:

Watch ye and pray, lest ye enter into temptation. The spirit truly is ready, but the flesh is weak.

Mark 14:28

Even Jesus himself was very prayerful while on earth. You might be wondering if Jesus needed prayer ? but he prayed regularly on the land, on the mountains, and every places he went to. Luke 6:12 says:

And it came to pass in those days, that he went out into a mountain to pray, and continued all night in prayer to God.

Even during his baptisms, he was praying. Luke 3:21.

Now when all the people were baptized, it came to pass, that Jesus also being baptized, and praying, the heaven was opened.

From the above scriptures, we can see that praying will make our heavens to open. The word says as Jesus was praying, the heaven was opened. This can mean many things as doors of opportunities and blessings from God to an answered prayer.

We are admonished to pray always as the word says in 1 Thessalonians 5:13 that:

Pray without ceasing

Prayer is very important as Christians because this is how we communicate with God. It is a form of humility and total dependency on God. If a person does not pray, its a form of pride telling God that you can do things by yourself. Now that you are saved or born again, God is now your father through Jesus Christ. As we know in the physical realm, we communicate with our parents. Prayer is that channel where we communicate with God our father. A Christian would not do well without being prayerful in his journey because we live in a wicked world full of demons and their agents in human forms.

One of the ways to pray effectively is to engage the Holy Spirit after your baptism in the Holy Ghost. The Scriptures says:

Likewise the Spirit also helpeth our infirmities: for we know not what we should pray for as we ought: but the Spirit itself maketh intercession for us with groanings which cannot be uttered.

Many times, you may not know what to pray about or how to pray it but if you engage the Holy Spirit, he would help you. And how do we engage the holy spirit in our prayer life ? By praying in the Spirit. The scriptures says:

But ye, beloved, building up yourselves on your most holy faith, praying in the Holy Ghost.

Jude 1:20

Therefore if you do not want to fail as a Christian, pray!

If you do not want to Fall as a Christian, pray!

And if you do not want to faint as a Christian, pray!

Evangelise

Now that you are saved and have been living as a Christian and being rooted and grounded in the faith, you will need to share your salvation, the love of Christ and the gospel in general to other people just as you have experienced yourself. By this way, you are not selfish and keeping your salvation to yourself but leading others to Jesus as well to be saved. This is called evangelism or soul winning. It is something Jesus commanded in Mark 16:15.

And he said unto them, Go ye into all the world, and preach the gospel to every creature.

This applies to every believers in Christ. It is a form of marketing Jesus and the love of God to reach other people who have not known him yet or reaching out to people to help them to be saved also.

In fact when you do this and get someone saved, you cause joy in heaven. This is what Jesus said in Luke 15:7:

I say unto you, that likewise joy shall be in heaven over one sinner that repenteth, more than over ninety and nine just persons, which need no repentance.

Anyone can be an evangelist to proclaim the gospel of Jesus Christ. You don't need a special calling or special anointing to evangelise Jesus. Just tell other people. It is as simple as that. 2 Timothy 4:5 says:

...do the work of an evangelist...

Soul winners are regarded as wise people. The scriptures says in Proverbs 11:30 that:

The fruit of the righteous is a tree of life;
and he that winneth souls is wise.

And what shall be the reward of a wise person ? The scriptures says:

The wise shall inherit glory:
but shame shall be the promotion of fools.

Proverbs 3:35

According to the scriptures, who are fools ? Let us see Psalms 14:1 that says:

The fool hath said in his heart, There is no God. They are corrupt, they have done abominable works...

A fool cannot share the love of God or of Christ Jesus because they are unbelievers anyway. They have no regard for God and say there is no God. In my personal experience of reaching out to the people out there about getting saved, I have heard all kinds of unbelievable things that people think or say about God. So far on two occasions, people have told me to spell the name of God backward and we know what that means. There are many other fearful things I have heard people said before in my personal experience. This shows the kind of heart some people have towards God. Some people would never accept you or your preaching, leave them and move to the next person. Some people would insult you, leave them and move to the next person, some would accuse you, but the fact is that they accused Jesus our Lord also while here on earth doing the work of his father. Do not be discouraged about what people say or do to you knowing that you are doing this for the Lord.

When it comes to evangelism, many Christians engaged in this right from ages past and many Churches conduct corporate evangelism where everyone go out together to proclaim the gospel. It is not a thing to be ashamed of. I personally have seen myself shared the gospel of Christ in divers places before and I intend to do more. Recently while in Paris France, I had to learn some French from a nearby person where I was reaching out to be able to tell people about Jesus and able to pronounce his name properly in French because I realized most people did not understand me in English. It is an interesting thing to be a soul winner! Jesus said:

Whosoever therefore shall be ashamed of me and of my words in this adulterous and sinful generation; of him also shall the Son of man be ashamed, when he cometh in the glory of his Father with the holy angels.

Mark 8:38

I'm sure you do not want to see Jesus to be ashamed of you at his appearance with his holy angels when the time comes just because you have not told other people about him or his word in this world while you are here. It would be a disastrous thing.

Now that you are saved, there are many other millions or billions of people that still need to be saved and it is our responsibilities as Christians to reach out to them in love by any means we can to get them saved as well. Paul the apostle said:

For though I preach the gospel, I have nothing to glory of: for necessity is laid upon me; yea, woe is unto me, if I preach not the gospel! For if I do this thing willingly, I have a reward: but if against my will, a dispensation of the gospel is committed unto me. What is my reward then? Verily that, when I preach the gospel, I may make the gospel of Christ without charge, that I abuse not my power in the gospel

1 Corinthians 9:16-18

There is a reward for every single soul we win to the Lord. Something such as this that causes joy is heaven definitely carries a heavy reward to whoever engages in it. It is wisdom to be a soul winner. It will make you to enjoy some benefits from God that other people do not just experience anyhow. God is faithful and he is a rewarder of those that diligently seek him.

But without faith it is impossible to please him: for he that cometh to God must believe that he is, and that he is a rewarder of them that diligently seek him.

Now that you are saved, go get other people saved and as you do with prayers before you go, the Lord will help you, work with you, confirm his word and even show signs as the scripture says in Mark 16:19 that:

And they went forth, and preached every where, the Lord working with them, and confirming the word with signs following. Amen.

And what is the reward for this ?

And Jesus answered and said, Verily I say unto you, There is no man that hath left house, or brethren, or sisters, or father, or mother, or wife, or children, or lands, for my sake, and the gospel's, But he shall receive an hundredfold now in this time, houses, and brethren, and sisters, and mothers, and children, and lands, with persecutions; and in the world to come eternal life.

Mark 10:29-30

Prepare for Eternity

Now that you are saved and have been living a Christian life from all you have read in the previous chapters, It is very important to focus and be preparing for heaven. This is the eternal home for every believers of Jesus Christ. It is our eternal place of rest to enjoy eternity with God our father. It is an experience never to miss after your salvation and after all you have done for the Lord while here on Earth.

Jesus said:

Let not your heart be troubled: ye believe in God, believe also in me. In my Father's house are many mansions: if it were not so, I would have told you. I go to prepare a place for you. And if I go and prepare a place for you, I will come again, and receive you unto myself; that where I am, there ye may be also.

John 14:1-3

We understand from the scriptures that Jesus is coming very soon. Times and events are showing how close we are to the rapture. It is something to be conscious of. Some Christians still don't believe that Heaven is real but we can see Jesus talking about Heaven in the scriptures because that is where he came from and that is where we are going if we do his will and not err away from the faith.

Jesus said again in Revelation 22:12 that:

And, behold, I come quickly; and my reward is with me, to give every man according as his work shall be.

Vs 16.
I Jesus have sent mine angel to testify unto you these things in the churches. I am the root and the offspring of David, and the bright and morning star.

I personally believe that the words of Jesus are to be taken very seriously the most because this is a person that came directly from God to tell us many things on the earth.

Never let anything on earth to distract your attention from heaven. The scriptures says:

If ye then be risen with Christ, seek those things which are above, where Christ sitteth on the right hand of God. Set your affection on things above, not on things on the earth

Colossians 3:1-2

Of course there are many other things to be doing daily and some regularly to keep your faith on fire such as:

Praying daily to God. Its a matter of "when" not "if". Jesus said:

But thou, when thou prayest, enter into thy closet, and when thou hast shut thy door, pray to thy Father which is in secret; and thy Father which seeth in secret shall reward thee openly.

Matthew 6:6

Obeying God and his word daily.

Living in love and not in hatred to other people no matter what they have done to you. Forgive and let go.

Living in Holiness and in peace with everyone. The scriptures says:

Follow peace with all men, and holiness, without which no man shall see the Lord.

Hebrews 12:14

Fasting to help you grow stronger spiritually. Its a matter of "when" also and not "if" Jesus said:

But thou, when thou fastest, anoint thine head, and wash thy face; That thou appear not unto men to fast, but unto thy Father which is in secret: and thy Father, which seeth in secret, shall reward thee openly.

Matthew 6:16

Taking the communion as often as possible. Jesus said:

He that eateth my flesh, and drinketh my blood, dwelleth in me, and I in him. As the living Father hath sent me, and I live by the Father: so he that eateth me, even he shall live by me. This is that bread which came down from heaven: not as your fathers did eat manna, and are dead: he that eateth of this bread shall live for ever.

John 6:56-58

Now that you are saved, it is important to do all these things to live a successful Christians life and to end up in heaven at the end of life or at the appearance of Jesus soon which is very important.

Finally, my brethren, be strong in the Lord, and in the power of his might.

Ephesians 6:10

Final Words

I believe you have been blessed reading this book. If so, pass it on to other people especially unbelievers, unsaved people, even new believers, new converts and new Christians in the faith to show them the love of God for their salvation as you have been saved also. Or for those already saved, for them to know the next steps after salvation.

I give all the Glory to God almighty my father, Jesus Christ my Master and lover and the Holy Spirit my helper and guide for helping me to write this book by divine inspirations to be a blessing to people all over the world extracting all the principles from his word. The Holy Scripture.

Other popular Christian books by me are:

Now That You Are Saved

PRIDE
AVOID IT
FOLO AJIBADE

FROM SPIRITUAL PERSPECTIVES BASED ON
CHRISTIAN FAITH

FOLO AJIBADE

For Partnership with our Gospel work to reach out to more people in distribution of books, tracts, leaflets, cds, media campaign, social media campaign and even TV & radio broadcasting

Visit our website at:

<u>https://www.kingdomdirect.org/partnership</u>

About the Author

Folo Ajibade is an author, prolific writer, an evangelist, a brother, speaker, adviser and a life coach. He is also the Founder and Director of Kingdom Direct Ministries based in the United Kingdom.

For more info, contact:

Email: info@kingdomdirect.org
Web: www.kingdomdirect.org

Social Media Contacts:

Facebook : https://facebook.com/kingdomdirectministries

Twitter : https://twitter.com/directkingdom   or   @directkingdom

Instagram: https://www.instagram.com/kingdomdirectministries/

Youtube : Kingdom Direct Ministries